In this little book, us a very good, l to the church both works. What's mo ourselves, as Christians, should do in our local church. This simple book may give you just the hope you need to go get involved in that local church that you've been considering.

Mark Dever
Pastor, Capitol Hill Baptist Church
Washington, D.C.

Jonathan Cruse's little introduction to the church would be a perfect book to give to new members, new converts, or anyone who wants to have a better idea of what the church is and what the church does. I know it would have been helpful if I had read this when I was a new Christian. The entire book is helpful, but especially encouraging is the final chapter on how to deal with the fact that the church consists of imperfect people. That chapter should be required reading for all church members.

Keith Mathison
Professor of Systematic Theology
Reformation Bible College, Sanford, Florida

A must read for every student! In this whistle-stop survey of church life, Jonathan winsomely opens our eyes to the wonderful, supernatural gift that God has given to His people and explains why it is vital for our flourishing. This is the perfect primer for all who are trying to grapple with the doctrine of the church. It will turn on the theological lights and help many appreciate their church in a new and meaningful way.

John T. Graham
Associate Minister, Hill Street Presbyterian Church, Lurgan, Northern Ireland

A STUDENT'S GUIDE TO CHURCH

JONATHAN LANDRY CRUSE

SERIES EDITORS:
JOHN PERRITT
& LINDA OLIVER

TRACK: DOCTRINE

Scripture quotations are from *The Holy Bible, English Standard Version*, copyright © 2001 by Crossway Bibles, a publishing ministry of Good News Publishers. Used by permission. All rights reserved. ESV Text Edition: 2011.

Copyright © Jonathan Landry Cruse 2025
paperback ISBN 978-1-5271-1284-1
ebook ISBN 978-1-5271-1309-1

10 9 8 7 6 5 4 3 2 1

First published in 2025
by
Christian Focus Publications Ltd,
Geanies House, Fearn, Ross-shire,
IV20 1TW, Great Britain
www.christianfocus.com

with

Reformed Youth Ministries,
1445 Rio Road East
Suite 201D
Charlottesville,
Virginia, 22911

Cover by MOOSE77
Printed by Gutenberg, Malta

All rights reserved. No part of this publication may be reproduced, stored in a retrieval system, or transmitted, in any form, by any means, electronic, mechanical, photocopying, recording or otherwise without the prior permission of the publisher or a licence permitting restricted copying. In the U.K. such licences are issued by the Copyright Licensing Agency, 4 Battlebridge Lane, London, SE1 2HX www.cla.co.uk

CONTENTS

Series Introduction 7

1. A Special People 9
2. A Cosmic Mission 19
3. A Glorious Worship 29
4. An Ordinary Service 37
5. A Godly Government 45
6. A Faithful Member 55
7. A Healthy Body 65
8. An Unfinished Work 73

Appendix A: Next Steps 83

Appendix B: Other Books on this Topic 85

To Levi, Lucy, Violet, Felicity, and Jude,

you are never too young to serve the church.

And to Him who said, "I will build my church."

Series Introduction

Christianity is a religion of words, because our God is a God of words. He created through words, calls Himself the Living Word, and wrote a book (filled with words) to communicate to His children. In light of this, pastors and parents should take great efforts to train the next generation to be readers. *Track* is a series designed to do exactly that.

Written for students, the *Track* series addresses a host of topics in three primary areas: Doctrine, Culture, and the Christian Life. *Track's* booklets are theologically rich, yet accessible. They seek to engage and challenge the student without dumbing things down.

One definition of a track reads: *a way that has been formed by someone else's footsteps.* The goal of the *Track* series is to point us to that 'someone else'—Jesus Christ. The One who forged a track to guide His followers. While we cannot follow this track perfectly, by His grace and Spirit He calls us to strive to stay on the path. It is our prayer that this series of books would help guide Christ's Church until He returns.

In His service,

John Perritt
RYM's Director of Resources
Series Co-Editor

Linda Oliver
RYM Ministry Associate
Series Co-Editor

1. A Special People

In my experience, most young people have one of two impressions of the church. For those who have grown up in the church, it is simply a given. It doesn't require much thought: at worst, it's a chore; at best, it simply is. For those who haven't grown up in the church, it is often seen as "that thing those people do." Likewise, arriving at this conclusion does not require a lot of intellectual strain. There is actually quite a bit of overlap in the two positions: the young person growing up in a Christian home doesn't think much about the church because they don't have a choice; the unbeliever doesn't think much about the church because it's out of sight and out of mind.

Therefore, in this little book, I want us to do something that might be completely new to you: let's *think* about the church. And let's make sure we have our thoughts guided by what the Bible says. The Bible actually has quite a lot to say about the church—a lot of *wonderful* things, in fact. I hope to unpack for you what I have come to learn over the years: the Bible presents the church as the greatest place on earth—*and it really is!*

DISCOVERING CHURCH

That realization began to dawn on me in my freshman year of college. I had moved far from home to study film at Temple University in Philadelphia, Pennsylvania. I knew practically no one at the school. I grew up in a small town and most of my graduating class stayed around to attend the local community college, or to go to the gigantic Penn State campus which was only about thirty minutes away. I opted to go to the other end of the state, and quickly discovered I was not up for it. I was terribly homesick. I had never spent much time away from home—I had never even been in a city before! For a while, all I wanted was to drop out and go home.

There were two things I had going for me: a recommendation of a solid church to attend, and a friend who would brave the scary subways with me to go each week. Although college is often a time of spiritual drifting for many young people, the Lord graciously did an opposite work in my life. Okay, there was still spiritual drifting at times (!), but it was never a church-less drifting. Although Monday through Saturday were quite hard the first semester or two, Sunday was always a highlight. I made friends immediately; I joined a choir (not really my thing, but it was a great way to connect); I even showed up early most weeks to attend both morning services. The Lord had made me hungry for His house: I wanted to be with the people, singing praises, and studying God's Word. My friend and I would prepare for a long afternoon, usually hanging out in one of the parks in Center City, so that we could return for the evening service and do it all over again. It was a long day, and logistically difficult, but it was the best day.

What I discovered was a felt reality of what the Bible teaches: *the church is the greatest place on earth.* That is because the church has a very unique relationship with God. The church is His special people. Indeed, I felt a special blessing from the Lord when I was in His house on His day with His people. Admittedly, this was sort of a surprise to me. Something that was just a given growing up was now great. To be clear, the church *is* great. Always. But now I saw it to be the case. In this book I want you to see it, too.

BOUGHT WITH THE BLOOD

What makes the church such a unique institution and the place of preeminent blessing is its relationship to God by virtue of the work of Jesus Christ. In Acts 20, we are told that the church belongs to God because He paid for it with the blood of His dear son: "the church of God, which he obtained with his own blood" (v. 28). Peter writes something similar when he says, "you were ransomed from the futile ways inherited from your forefathers, not with perishable things such as silver or gold, but with the precious blood of Christ, like that of a lamb without blemish or spot" (1 Pet. 1:18-19).

Immediately, our estimation of church should be raised when we consider it could not even exist were it not for the death of Christ on the cross. The value of the church demands that we hold it dear and precious to us. Admittedly, that value may not be apparent from our human perspective, but this is why we need the Scriptures: we need to see the church for how God sees it. And to God, we are "a chosen race, a royal priesthood, a holy nation, a people for his own possession, that you may proclaim the excellencies of him who called you out of darkness into his marvelous light. Once you were not a people, but now you are God's people; once you had not received mercy, but now you have received mercy" (1 Peter 2:9-10).

The church, therefore, is the people of God who belong to Him, not by virtue of creation, but by virtue of salvation. We could say that, although everyone belongs to God because He is their Maker, the church *doubly* belongs to God because He is their Maker *and* their Savior. Although this should enforce a sense of indebtedness to the Lord and instill within all believers a desire to serve and obey Him, it should also give a sense of privilege, dignity, and worth. Moses told Israel the same thing: "Happy are you, O Israel! Who is like you, a people saved by the LORD" (Deut. 33:29). The heart is full and the head held high when you belong to the church, as it is the special society of those who have been saved by the Lord.

CALLED-OUT ONES

The Greek word that is translated "church" in the New Testament underscores this idea. It literally means "the called-out ones." The church is the people that God has called out from this world which is fading away and has instead brought into His eternal family. The church is the people who have been especially chosen by God for "blessings without number and mercies without end."[1]

My four-year-old daughter's bed has helped me understand this privilege. Let me explain. She has countless stuffed animals ("stuffies") at the foot of her bed—seriously, there are far too many, and she may be soon at risk of drowning in plush! But even so, it's only her precious white stuffed doggy that gets to come up to the head of the bed, snuggle under her arm, and "sleep" with her. They have been called out from the rest, and it's a sign of my daughter's love for these particular few that she bestows such a privilege on them. This idea of a gracious choice is built into the very word *church*: they are the people that God has set apart from the world, called out of sin and hell to enjoy the blessings of salvation with Him forever.

Theologians will sometimes clarify further this idea of the church—which is synonymous with the elect—by referring to it as *the invisible church*. This simply means it's the church that is invisible, or hidden, from human perception

---

[1] Michael A. Perry, "O God beyond All Praising," 1982.

(since we do not know who is truly saved or not), though it is known entirely and eternally to God. The Westminster Confession of Faith says that the invisible church "consists of the whole number of the elect, that have been, are, or shall be gathered into one, under Christ the Head thereof; and is the spouse, the body, the fullness of him that filleth all in all." Calling the church the "spouse" of Christ is a nod to Ephesians 5:25 where we read, "Husbands, love your wives, *as Christ loved the church and gave himself up for her.*" When used in this way, the term "church" speaks of all Christians (see also Acts 20:28).

But we can also speak of *the visible church*, which describes the church as you and I see it. This is the church that is found the whole world over, in any denomination, wherever people faithfully confess that Jesus Christ is Lord. Though the invisible church only consists of true believers, the visible church consists of all those who *say* they are believers. Paul writes about this universal expression of the visible church: "all those who in every place call upon the name of our Lord Jesus Christ, both their Lord and ours" (1 Cor. 1:2).

So, if you are looking through your theological lens, zoom out as far as possible, get a panoramic view that encompasses all eternity, and you will "see" the invisible church. Zoom in further to capture the globe, and you are looking at the visible church. But we can zoom in further still, to a particular city or town, and we find *the local church*. Another term for this is congregation. You probably have more than one wherever you live. When Paul writes, "To the church of the Thessalonians in God the Father and the Lord Jesus Christ," he is writing to a local church (1 Thess. 1:1). The local church is a discernible group of people that meet in a specific location. The story I just relayed about my experience with a church in Philadelphia was a story about falling in love with a *local* church. That's what we are going to be focusing on in this book, too.

The local church is where the rubber meets the road, so to speak. It's where everything that the Bible says about the church comes to life. So, in the pages that follow, we are going to consider the mission of the local church, the way it functions, and the role you are to play in all of it.

MAIN POINT:

The church is the special people of God who belong to Him because Christ died for them. There is no privilege greater in all of life than to belong to the church.

QUESTIONS FOR REFLECTION:

- What is your experience with church? Did you grow up in one?
- Is the idea of church exciting to you? Why or why not?
- What makes the church so precious in God's eyes?

2. A Cosmic Mission

In the last chapter we gave at least an initial answer to the question of what the church is. Now we ask: What does the church *do*? Opinions abound on this important question, but it seems to me the Bible is pretty clear. Let me first suggest an answer, and then we will explore some passages that develop the idea further. *The mission of the church is to be a faithful outpost of God's heavenly kingdom on earth.*

LOOK OUT, HELL!

This will mean a variety of things. One of them is that the church, when true to its mission, is the primary means Christ uses to advance His cause in the world and crush the strongholds of Satan and sin.

In Matthew 16:18—one of the primary passages about the mission of the church—Jesus announces, "I will build my church, and the gates of hell shall not prevail against it." The important thing to glean from this verse is the active, offensive nature of the church's mission. Jesus does not say that the gates of heaven will not crumble to the onslaught of evil (though that is certainly true). Rather, it is the defensive strongholds of evil that He has in His sights. In other words, God is going to launch an attack against all that is evil—and the church is the means by which He carries it out! To belong to the church is to belong to God's work in the world of fighting sin and conquering the evil attempts of Satan to overcome His plan. Did you know the church was involved in something so—and I mean this in the truest sense of the term—*awesome*?

Notice also that the successful mission of the church is inevitable. Jesus guarantees that He is overseeing this battle plan: "*I* will build *my* church," He says. No wonder the gates of hell will not prevail against the church—when has any work that God gets behind failed? It is the church, therefore, that gets to be on the front lines of God's *victorious* conquest. What a thrill!

Although sin and wickedness have the effect of decaying and darkening all that is good, Jesus says the church counters those effects by being "the salt of the earth" and "the light of the world" (Matt. 5:13, 14). Jesus uses the metaphor of salt which, particularly in the ancient world, was used as a preservative for other foods. The church is God's salt, used to preserve and protect the world from the destructive forces of evil. Likewise, the church is to be the light of God's glory that sends the shadows of sin fleeing. Though involvement in the church might initially seem quite mundane, the Bible suggests it is anything but. The church is where you go to play a part in the inevitable defeat of the devil. The church is where you go be a victor: "thanks be to God, who in Christ always leads us in triumphal procession" (2 Cor. 2:14).

OUR MARCHING ORDERS

Now, if that's what the church exists for, how does it happen? How do we actually advance the cause of Christ, shine the light of heaven, and stamp out the powers of hell? The answer might surprise you. In one of the most well-known passages in the whole Bible, Jesus tells His disciples the battle strategy for the church: "All authority in heaven and on earth has been given to me. Go therefore and make disciples of all nations, baptizing them in the name of the Father and of the Son and of the Holy

Spirit, teaching them to observe all that I have commanded you. And behold, I am with you always, to the end of the age" (Matt. 28:18-20).

If you were expecting swords or sniper rifles, sorry to disappoint. As Paul reminds us, "We do not wrestle against flesh and blood, but against the rulers, against the authorities, against the cosmic powers over this present darkness, against the spiritual forces of evil in the heavenly places" (Eph. 6:12). "Rulers" and "authorities" is Paul-speak for demonic forces. Since the church's enemy is a spiritual one, her weapons are spiritual, too. Hence, when Jesus gives the mission statement of the church, armaments and ammo are absent. Instead, He speaks of spiritual formation.

The church is called to go into the world and "*make disciples.*" We are called to speak—not even to shout, but simply to tell. That's because this discipling mission requires instruction in the ways of the Lord ("teaching them to observe all that I have commanded you"). Furthermore, that instruction is meant to take place in the life and fellowship of a local church (hence, the mission first to baptize disciples—more on this in chapter four). In other words, the church gains victory over her enemies, not by conquering them, but by converting them.

For some people, perhaps this sounds more terrifying than all-out combat! But even as we are called to faithfully witness to the Lord Jesus, He again promises us assured victory through His abiding presence: "And behold, I am with you always, to the end of the age." One of the places we find proof of this profound promise is in the Book of Acts. There, we read about the multiplication of disciples, starting in Jerusalem and then reaching to the far-flung places of the then-known world. Men who should be fearful are faithful; those who would be otherwise timid are bold in the face of a mocking and persecuting world. Because Jesus is with them, they preach. And as the Word goes, the church grows: "And the word of God continued to increase, and the number of the disciples multiplied greatly" (Acts 6:7). One thinks of the brilliant response the Reformer Martin Luther gave when asked how it was he caused such an amazing revival in sixteenth-century Germany: "I did nothing … The Word did everything."

THE CHURCH'S WEAPON

Therefore, the Word of God is our weapon, and our watchword is "go and tell." Though dull to human eyes, when wielded by Spirit-empowered saints of God, it is "sharper than any two-edged sword," with the ability to pierce people right to their heart (Heb. 4:12). The proclamation of the good news of Jesus' death and resurrection convicts, converts, and consoles. It does everything necessary to accomplish God's purposes in the world, and thus has been given to the church to wield. The Word of God has been entrusted to us as our "good deposit" (2 Tim. 1:14) and the church is therefore called "a pillar and buttress of the truth" (1 Tim. 3:15). Says one author, "The truth is [the church's] mission. The truth is her message. The truth is her reason for existing in the world."[2]

Think about that for a moment. Before you dismiss this as unimpressive, think about how critical truth is in our day and age. Our culture is awash in a sea of subjectivity—no one is willing to defend objective, universal truths. Instead, the ultimate arbiter is placed in each individual: every person gets to chart out their own course and determine their own values. Unhinging our lives from traditional values or so-called

---

[2] Dustin Benge, *The Loveliest Place: The Beauty and Glory of the Church* (Wheaton, IL: Crossway, 2022), 78.

objective truths is the first step in the process of going "woke." While this move was meant to liberate people, it has done quite the opposite. Countless millions are imprisoned in an anxious cell of their own making, never certain if they have done enough to be happy, constantly angry at anyone who dares not affirm them. Maybe you have friends who have followed the promise of expressive individualism—a life that prioritizes knowing and expressing yourself as the means to personal happiness—to find that is has not offered the sort of security and satisfaction they were hoping. Maybe that's your experience as well. TikToks and Instagram reels showcase influencers who promise a better path forward, but it's all vanity and deceit. Being true to yourself ("you do you") is an attractive proposition, but ultimately an empty one. If this is the path the world has gone down, what is the most important thing the church could do? Simply, the answer is: *tell the truth*. The Word of God, which comes from outside of us and stands authoritatively over us, gives the direction and answers that every sinner so desperately needs. The church exists to make that Word known.

THE CHURCH AND GOD'S WISDOM

A perennial problem for the church is believing that the center of our mission is really something as simple as proclamation. It's hard to accept that something like the Bible is sufficient to do all that we are called to do. It can appear to be so ... *simple.* Surely, God has bigger things in store for us than just this! That sentiment exposes a deficient understanding of God's Word. To use a humorous example, the church can often behave like Agent J, Will Smith's character from *Men in Black* (does that age me?). He pouts that when he joins the elite alien-fighting crew he is only armed with a puny-looking pistol, called The Noisy Cricket. Everyone else gets impressive shotgun-like blasters. However, The Noisy Cricket packs such a punch that the first time he uses it he is sent soaring backwards in the air. There was more to that weapon than met the eye.

There is more to the Word than we realize. There is therefore more to the church than we realize. The church does not have the odds stacked against her when her weapon is the Word of God—quite the opposite, in fact. "We preach Christ crucified, a stumbling block to Jews and folly to Gentiles, but to those who are called, both Jews and Greeks, Christ the power of God and the wisdom of God. For the foolishness of God is wiser than men, and the weakness of God is stronger than men" (1 Cor. 1:23-25).

As foolish as it might seem to us, it is in God's infinite wisdom that the church would be His plan for world history. Paul writes that "through the church the manifold wisdom of God might now be made known to the rulers and authorities in the heavenly places." (Eph. 3:10). The spiritual forces have a better grasp on the relevancy of the church than many believers do! To them it has been revealed that God's perfect plan unfolds through the church. Let's learn the lesson, too. If you want to be a part of God's inevitably victorious work in the world, you must be part of His church.

MAIN POINT:
The church stands central in God's glorious and victorious work in the world, and you can't afford to miss out on it.

QUESTIONS FOR REFLECTION:
- How would you answer this question: What is the mission of the church?

CHURCH

- Do you think of the church as participating in the cosmic battle between good and evil?
- What hope does the church have in fulfilling the difficult calling she has received?

3. A Glorious Worship

There is nothing that God wants more from His church than her worship. Jesus makes the astounding statement that "the hour is coming, and is now here, when the true worshipers will worship the Father in spirit and truth, for the Father is seeking such people to worship him" (John 4:23). God is after people who will truly and faithfully worship Him on the earth—and the church is that group of people! As we have seen, the church is the very special people of God. Part of our unique privilege is to be "a royal priesthood"—a people whose very calling is to offer a sacrifice of praise (1 Pet. 2:10; Heb. 13:15). The church is sometimes referred to as the temple of God (Eph. 2:21; 1 Pet. 2:5)—just as the temple was the center of worship in the Old Testament, the church is now the center of worship in the New Covenant era.

The name "church" also hints at the primacy of worship. Recall that in Greek "church" means "called-out ones." The Old Testament equivalent of the term is usually translated "assembly," and the point of God's people assembling in the Old Testament was always to worship (e.g., Ps. 22:22, 26:12). To be in the assembly was to be in worship. To be part of the church is to be part of a worshiping community. This is why we exist. In other words, we are called out from the world to assemble together in order to glorify the name of God.

Without worship, a church is nothing. And if a church does not prioritize worship, the other good things that she may attempt will be weakened. We were made to worship. It's the most important thing we can do on earth. And even in glory, it's what we will be doing.

WITH REVERENCE AND YAWN?

Okay, I get it. You are not very excited. Church worship might not seem to be the most glamorous thing in the world. You understand that the church is made to worship, but that doesn't necessarily make it anymore appealing to you. Duty and delight don't always go together, at least not right away.

I am sure some of you would rather sleep in on Sundays, or do any number of other important things. Perhaps the music isn't really your thing, or the preacher doesn't have your favorite style, and so the draw to come on Sundays isn't very great. Church leaders feel that pressure. They are always looking for ways to get people in the doors, even their own members! So, sometimes what churches will do is try to make their worship a really impressive "experience"—lights, videos, professional sound design, catchy music, the whole nine yards.

What these Christians are missing is an understanding of the supernatural reality that is taking place when the church assembles for worship. If you grasp what the Bible says happens in corporate worship, you wouldn't ever be bored. You would also see that the attempts to make worship cool and exciting are completely unnecessary—the most exciting thing in the world is taking place in worship, and it is something that no human beings could ever manufacture. What is it? *Meeting with God!*

A DIVINE ENCOUNTER

A fascinating conversation-starter I like to use when hanging with a group of people is to ask, "Who is the most famous person you have ever met?" Some really amazing stories have come from that question.[3] However, no one has yet offered the answer that is true for every worshiping Christian: we have met God Himself.

Did you know that's what happens every Sunday, all over the world? The Old Testament saints understood that was the high point of worship. That's why they called the tabernacle "the tent of meeting" (e.g. Exod. 27:21). We don't have a tabernacle anymore, but we have something better: in Hebrews, we are told that through worship we are actually, as it were, lifted into heaven itself to meet with God there. Listen to this breath-taking explanation of what happens when we worship: "you have come to Mount Zion and to the city of the living God, the heavenly Jerusalem, and to innumerable angels in festal gathering, and to the assembly of the firstborn who are enrolled in heaven, and to God, the judge of all, and to the spirits of the righteous made perfect, and to Jesus, the mediator of a new covenant" (Heb. 12:22-24).

To me, those two three-word clauses snuck into the middle of the passage are some of

---

[3] For me, if you're wondering, I sat in front of Jimmy Carter at a baseball game once.

the greatest understatements in all of the Bible: "and to God... and to Jesus"—*what?!* Could it really be that we come into the very presence of God when we worship? Yes! The Bible is replete with other indications that this is what happens in worship. For example, in the Old Testament, another phrase that was synonymous for worship was "before the Lord." That is, if someone was coming "before the Lord," they were doing so in an act of worship (look at 2 Samuel 6, where the phrase is used numerous times). Or consider how Jesus says, "Where two or three are gathered in my name, there am I among them" (Matt. 18:20).

Now, one of the foundational doctrines of the nature of God is His omnipresence, the fact that He is everywhere, all the time, always. That might seem to suggest that we are saying nothing special at all to say we meet with God in worship. But there is an important distinction to be made: although God is everywhere present, He is present in a special way in worship. Worship is sort of like His office hours. A professor is always a professor, day and night and weekends. However, if you phoned up your professor on Saturday night to ask a question about the upcoming exam, he would tell you to visit him instead during one of his office hours. This is when a professor promises to engage with his students and give them the help they need. The worship services of God's church are that special, particular time where God invites His people into His very presence and meets them with grace.

MISSING OUT

If that is all true (and it is), can you really afford to miss out on worship? A better question: would you even *want* to? If you could, would you want to meet the strongest person in the universe? What about the smartest? You don't have to go to a Guinness Book of World Records convention—you just have to go to church.

This also means that if what we get in church is nothing less than God Himself, what need is there to make church "cool"? How can lights or music compete with a one-on-one meeting with the creator of the world? He is enough to make church relevant. He is enough to make church thrilling. He is enough to make church awesome. Are you there?

There is a great anxiety that plagues many young people who spend any amount of time on social media: the fear of missing out (FOMO). We see our friends posting pictures of cool hangouts, fun parties, awesome vacations, and we get a sense that our lives are somehow lackluster because we weren't a part of it. In the main, FOMO is a really unhealthy thing: it breeds on jealousy and pride. But there is a healthy and holy FOMO that I want to instill in you. Dear reader, let me be as abundantly clear as I can be: if you are not in worship, you are missing out on the greatest thing this world has to offer. Indeed, it's the greatest thing that God has to offer. There is nothing more tragic than to have that opportunity before you and to not take it.

MAIN POINT:

Worship is the most important thing we could ever do, and the church is the primary place to do it.

QUESTIONS FOR REFLECTION:

- How would you describe how you feel about your church's worship?
- How can we say that God meets us in worship?
- What would you say to someone who says, "I don't need church. I can worship God alone at my home"?

4. An Ordinary Service

In the previous chapter we learned that what makes worship so exciting is that we are meeting with the Lord Himself. As we do, He speaks to us and even permits us to speak back to Him! There is a divine dialogue that is taking place in the church's worship.

While that is a breathtaking thought, the way the conversation is structured is pretty simple and ordinary. God speaks to us through the reading and preaching of His Word, as well as through the administration of the sacraments of baptism and the Lord's Supper. We primarily speak back to God in our prayers (which includes singing). These elements—the Word, sacraments, and prayer—are often called the "ordinary means of grace": simple things which are used as the conduit, or instrument, to bring the benefits and blessings of Christ to His people. These ordinary means constitute the sum and substance of the church's worship. In the remainder of this chapter, we will consider each in turn.

THE WORD

We have already considered how the Word of God is indispensable in the mission of the church. Therefore, it follows that the Word is indispensable to the church's worship, too. We are given a little window into church life in the early days of the first church in Jerusalem, and we are told that the people gathered regularly together and "devoted themselves to the apostles' teaching" (Acts 2:42). The church's commitment to the Word of God is on account of what God does by His Word. Our God is a speaking God. There was a time when there was nothing—and then God spoke (Gen. 1:4). And just as God is able to speak the world into existence, He is able to speak life into existence into otherwise dead souls (2 Cor. 4:6). The prophet Ezekiel learned that lesson when God took him to a graveyard, commanding him to bring the dead bones there to life simply by saying, "Hear the word of the Lord" (Ezek. 37:4). God's method of salvation is clear: "faith comes from hearing, and hearing through the word of Christ" (Rom. 10:17).

But the Word of God is not just for conversion. The Westminster Shorter Catechism teaches that "The Spirit of God maketh the reading, but especially the preaching, of the word, an effectual means of convincing and converting sinners, *and of building them up in holiness and comfort, through faith, unto salvation*" (89). When the church prioritizes God's Word in worship, God's people are called away from their sin, comforted by the grace of the gospel, and guided by divine wisdom for all of life. Further, when we make God's Word the primary focus of our worship, we can be assured that our worship is pleasing to Him. Thus, the church should read, preach, sing, and pray God's Word. "Let the word of Christ dwell in you richly" is God's instruction to the worshiping church (Col. 3:16).

Maybe you need to rethink your estimation of churches that read a lot of Scripture and have sermons that go longer than fifteen or twenty minutes. It's not meant to be boring; it's a blessing.

SACRAMENTS

There are two sacraments which have been entrusted to the church to observed until the return of Christ: baptism and the Lord's Supper.

The word sacrament comes from the Latin word *sacramentum* which means "mystery." This is a useful word, not because we are in the dark about what a sacrament is, but because the nature of how a sacrament works is beyond us. In that sense, it is properly mysterious. R. C. Sproul said, "In its most rudimentary form, the idea of the sacrament involves an experience of something that is sacred—something that we regard as extraordinary or uncommon, something with a special meaning or significance attached to it."[4] So although the things we use in the sacraments (water for baptism and bread and wine for the Lord's Supper) are very ordinary, what the Lord does through them is anything but.

Baptism

In baptism, the Lord symbolizes and seals (or guarantees) to His people that they have been cleansed from their sins and belong to Him. "Do you not know that all of us who have been baptized into Christ Jesus were baptized into his death? We were buried therefore with him by baptism into death, in order that, just as

---

4   R. C. Sproul, "What Is a Sacrament?" https://www.ligonier.org/learn/articles/what-is-a-sacrament

Christ was raised from the dead by the glory of the Father, we too might walk in newness of life" (Rom. 6:3-4). So, while the church *shares* the good news through preaching, the church can also *show* the good news in baptism. That is, one of its primary aims is to confirm to God's people what His Word says: we really are cleansed and forgiven when we believe in Jesus. In the same way that washing something with water makes it clean, believing on Christ makes you new.

Baptism is also something like the official entry into the church, which is really clear in the book of Acts (see also Matt. 28:19). Why is this the case? Through baptism, our union with Christ is symbolized, but so is our union and communion with other believers. So, Paul will say in 1 Corinthians 12, "For in one Spirit we were all baptized into one body—Jews or Greeks, slaves or free" (v. 13). The church is made up of people who are very different from one another, but baptism shows that we share in the one Christ. If we all have Jesus, then there is more in common to keep us together than differences could keep us apart. One author says, "Baptism is a countercultural act, almost a form of protest. Beyond everything else that tries to define us—our career, our citizenship, our status as consumers in a market economy—baptism locates our primary identity in the body of Christ."[5] That's a really important thing for the church to remember. And this is why baptism is part of the church's public worship services, and not something that Christians should do privately at their home or at camp with their friends. It's about being in the body of Christ, the church.

The Lord's Supper

The Lord's Supper also symbolizes and seals the promises of the gospel. Jesus said that bread represents His body which is broken for us and wine represents His blood which is poured out for us (see Luke 22:19-20). As a sign, the Supper points us back to the cross as the fundamental aspect of the Christian's faith and hope. Most amazingly, Jesus says that what He did on the cross is "for you." What took place on the cross was for our direct benefit. We may forget that, but the Supper has been given to the church as a perpetual reminder of the blessings of the gospel which belong directly to us.

---

5   Philip Graham Ryken, *City on a Hill* (Chicago, IL: Moody Publishers, 2003), 76.

An Ordinary Service

Like baptism, the Lord's Supper also helps us to understand what a wondrous thing the church is. As we share a meal, we remember that the church is our family. God has brought us all together to share in His love. He gives us not only Himself in the Supper, but He gives us each other! "The cup of blessing that we bless, is it not a participation in the blood of Christ? The bread that we break, is it not a participation in the body of Christ? Because there is one bread, we who are many are one body, for we all partake of the one bread" (1 Cor. 10:16-17).

PRAYER

It is a sign of people's pride and inflated sense of self-importance when they are only interested in speaking and never listening. It is disheartening to be in a conversation with someone who never thinks to ask you a question but only wants to share their opinion. Remarkably, the great and mighty Lord is not too important to listen to us. In worship, we are having a conversation with God, and it goes two ways! If God speaks to us through His Word and sacraments, we speak back through prayers and praises. This is how we tell the Lord how much we love and adore Him, how we show Him that His Word is on our hearts, and even how we can let Him know the struggles we have and ask for His help. Prayer is a means of grace because it gives us access to our gracious God through Jesus Christ: "Let us then with confidence draw near to the throne of grace, that we may receive mercy and find grace to help in time of need" (Heb. 4:16). The church is to be a "house of prayer" (see Isa. 56:7), because God loves to hear the prayers of His people (1 Pet. 3:12).

MAIN POINT:
What should make up the bulk of the church's worship is the reading and preaching of God's Word, the sacraments, and prayer, because these are all things that God has promised to use to grow us in grace.

QUESTIONS FOR REFLECTION:
- Why are the Word, sacraments, and prayer called "ordinary means of grace"?
- Have you been baptized? Does it matter?
- Does your church pray in worship? How often, and what are the specific types of prayers that are offered up?

5. A Godly Government

I write this as my country is nearing the end of an intense presidential election season. That means I have recently been inundated with ads for each candidate, and many of them are the kind that attack the opposing side with claims of incompetency and corruption. I also get a text message from an unknown number every few hours asking if I have registered to vote. This can make anyone want to throw in the towel on the idea of government, but we all recognize the essential nature of leadership. Complain all we want: without official governance our societies would devolve into chaos.

The same is true in the church. And while Christ is the head of the church (Col. 1:19), He has also appointed individuals to be His ambassadors on earth, who can mediate His heart and mind to properly guide a local congregation. They are called elders and deacons, and they exist for your good. Therefore, it's important that you know a little about them.

ELDERS

When Titus was planting a church in Crete, Paul underscored the absolute necessity of finding and establishing elders to lead the nascent congregation. He writes, "This is why I left you in Crete, so that you might put what remained into order, and appoint elders in every town as I directed you" (Titus 1:5). In Greek, it's more like "that you might straighten what's out of joint still." The idea is that the appointment of elders will help correct issues in a local church. Without them, things are going to be out of whack—and that includes you and me! We are so wayward by nature that we need the wise correction and soul-shepherding of elders in the church.

There are two distinct functions in the office of elder. Paul instructs Timothy, "Let the elders who rule well be considered worthy of *double honor*, especially those who labor in preaching and teaching" (1 Tim. 5:17). This implies that while all elders are called to rule, only some labor in preaching and teaching. Some churches will distinguish between ruling elders and teaching elders. Pastors are teaching elders, but there should be emphasis on elders. In other words, the pastor of the church is not the president or the chairman of the church. Human sin is too insidious to entrust the leadership of the church to a single individual. Rather, pastors are elders who focus especially on leading a church through the public and private teaching of the Bible, but all elders together commit to watching over the spiritual needs of the congregation. Hebrews 13 instructs us, "Obey your leaders and submit to them, for they are keeping watch over your souls, as those who will have to give an account" (v. 17).

Elders in a church join with Christ, and represent Christ, to God's people by leading them through the difficulties of life and the challenges of holiness in accordance with God's Word. That is why elders are referred to as under-shepherds. Jesus Christ is the "chief Shepherd" (1 Pet. 5:4) and the "Overseer of our souls" (1 Pet. 2:25). The elders' responsibility is carefully to steward the souls that belong to Him, representing His kingly care and gracious love to the church.

At times, this will mean the unpleasant business of exercising church discipline to rebuke sin in the life of a congregant and thereby maintain the honor of Christ and the purity of His church. While some denominations believe this is a responsibility of the whole church (for example, congregational meetings need to be held and votes taken to admit anyone into membership or excommunicate them from membership), other denominations, particularly Presbyterians, see this as a duty entrusted to the elders of the church. Elders are called to "rule" and to "lead" (1 Tim. 5:17; Heb. 13:7), and one of the primary ways they do that is through these sorts of disciplinary acts. They are something like sentries stationed outside of the church: Christ has given them the authority to admit people into the church, but also, if necessary, to keep people out (see Matt. 16:19, 18:16-19; John 20:23).

DEACONS

God establishes the church in such a way that not only our spiritual needs are met, but even our physical ones are met, too. The people who are entrusted with this responsibility are called deacons. We learn about the institution of this office in Acts 6:

> *Now in these days when the disciples were increasing in number, a complaint by the Hellenists arose against the Hebrews because their widows were being neglected in the daily distribution. And the twelve summoned the full number of the disciples and said, "It is not right that we should give up preaching the word of God to serve tables. Therefore, brothers, pick out from among you seven men of good repute, full of the Spirit and of wisdom, whom we will appoint to this duty. (Acts 6:1-3)*

Apparently, an attempt at a ministry to the poor was not working out well in the early church. The believing widows needed food, and they were not getting any. What were the apostles to do? Notice what they don't do: they don't turn them away by saying, "If you're hungry, pray harder!" The early church did not try to over-spiritualize things to the point of saying that our physical needs are unimportant. And so, they established the office of deacon, which in Greek means "servant"—it is an office that is designed especially to come to your aid in the relief of physical troubles. The church today must follow that same pattern.

Yes, our physical needs are secondary to our spiritual needs, undoubtedly. But they are still needs. They are still important. It makes me think of Shakespeare's famous lines from *The Merchant of Venice*: "If you prick us, do we not bleed? If you tickle us, do we not laugh? If you poison us, do we not die?"[6] That's you and me, isn't it? If we lose a job, do we not still have bills to pay? If our car breaks down, do we not still have to get around town? If we fall terribly ill, do we have to get to the doctor? Yes, yes, yes! We are alive in the Spirit, but we are embodied here on earth, where we will face difficulties with our health, or finances, or living situation. That matters to God, and therefore it matters to the church. The Scriptures never promote a sort of gnostic dualism that detaches our spiritual experience from our physical reality. The two are very much intertwined. God created both our body and our soul and He cares for both our body and our soul—and part of the way He shows that continual care is through the office of deacon. The office was created and constituted because we have very real needs that matter.

---

6   William Shakespeare, *The Merchant of Venice*, Act 3, Scene 1.

REPRESENTATIVES OF CHRIST

Pastors, elders, and deacons are representatives of Christ to the church on earth. Pastors showcase Christ as the great prophet who teaches us God's Word. Elders point us to the kingly reign of Christ, who governs all things well. Deacons remind us of our merciful high priest, who intercedes to God for our needs. But the Bible makes something really clear about leaders in a local church: they are to represent Jesus not just in their work but in their very lives.

There are a few places in the Bible where we are given qualifications individuals need to meet before they could properly fulfill the office of elder or deacon. The interesting thing about these qualifications is that they have very little to do with giftedness and have everything to do with godliness. We are not told, for example, that elders must be successful businessmen, particularly skilled in administration, adept at handling conflict, or creative and visionary leaders (though none of these things would be bad in an elder!). Instead, we are told that "an overseer, as God's steward, must be above reproach. He must not be arrogant or quick-tempered or a drunkard or violent or greedy for gain, but hospitable, a lover of good, self-controlled, upright, holy, and disciplined" (Titus 1:7-8). Similarly, deacons "must be dignified, not double-tongued, not addicted to much wine, not greedy for dishonest gain. They must hold the mystery of the faith with a clear conscience." (1 Tim. 3:8-9).

All of this points to the fact that it is God who rules His church, not man. Therefore, those who steward it are to be, before and above anything else, *godly!* We also believe that the Lord will lead each congregation by His Spirit to find these sorts of leaders. Although congregations choose their elders and deacons (see again the instructions for finding deacons in Acts 6:3), ultimately it is Christ working through the people to bring them the servant-leaders He desires. And since our gracious Savior Jesus Christ is head of the church, we should have every confidence to trust that the rule and government of the church will be for our good.

MAIN POINT:
Church leadership consists of elders and deacons, offices that, when filled by the right individuals, reflect the whole of Jesus' heart for His people.

QUESTIONS FOR REFLECTION:

- Read Acts 6, 1 Timothy 3, Titus 1, and 1 Peter 5: what other qualifications for elders and deacons do you find here?
- In what ways are elders and deacons meant to represent Jesus to the church?
- Why is church discipline sometimes necessary?

6. A Faithful Member

Commitment has fallen on tough times in recent decades. One online dating website recently found in a survey of its users that commitment was the greatest fear for millennials considering a relationship. I can only imagine that fear—"commitment phobia"—has increased for subsequent generations. We don't like to be tied down. We want to keep our options open. We are afraid that there might be something better out there.

This has bled into the way people view many aspects of life, including church. Many people live as "church hoppers"—going from one place to the next as it fancies them. Others, even if they stick with one church, keep a loose association with it—attending now and then, but remaining on the fringes and never the center of church life.

WHY FORMAL MEMBERSHIP?

That means that the idea of church membership is a hard concept to get behind. In my pastoral experience, I am regularly trying to convince people of the necessity (and blessing!) of committing to a local church. One of the common arguments I get is that church membership is not in the Bible. Is that true, though?

Though the Bible never specifically gives instruction for formal church membership, the concept can be found all over the place. It is the logical corollary of church leadership, which we considered in the previous chapter. Peter tells elders to "shepherd the flock of God that is among you" (1 Pet. 5:2)—this indicates that there was a particular group of people that the elders knew they had a responsibility for. Likewise, we read that Christians are to "remember your leaders, those who spoke to you the word of God. Consider the outcome of their way of life, and imitate their faith" (Heb. 13:7). They are not to imitate *any* leaders, but *their* leaders. The way that leaders know who to lead, and believers know who to follow, is through formal membership and affiliation within a local church.

When Paul writes to churches, he knows who he is writing to. He knows that Euodia and Synteche are part of the Philippian church (Phil. 4:2). He knows that Phoebe goes to the church in Cenchreae, and that Urbanus and Stachys are in Rome (Rom. 16:1, 9). There is a congregation that meets at Nympha's house, which is distinct from the congregation that meets in Philemon's house, and these are separate from the church at someone else's house (we're not told whose) in Laodicea (see Col. 4:15-16 and Philem. 2). The point is this: the church is not just an amorphous association of random people who happen to show up on the same day in the same place at the same time. The church is a definable group of Christians who have made a commitment to follow Jesus together. It's a formal and a public association, and that's why pastors know who to lead, members know who to follow, and Paul knows to whom he's writing!

WHAT IS FAITHFUL MEMBERSHIP?

What I want to think through with you in the remainder of this chapter (and the next) is what church membership requires of you. What is expected of you if you commit yourself to the local church? Let's think through just five things.

Attend

The first is obvious, I hope. You need to attend church. There is no way you can meaningfully benefit from all the blessings of the church if you are not there! We will have any number of reasons to shirk church worship and gatherings, but the Bible is clear: "Enter his gates with thanksgiving, and his courts with praise!" (Ps. 100:4). Doing that requires leaving your house. God expects His people to worship Him together.

Coming together is not only for the glory of God, but also for the mutual benefit of church members. Hebrews 10:24-25 says, "And let us consider how to stir up one another to love and good works, *not neglecting to meet together*, as is the habit of some, but encouraging one another, and all the more as you see the Day drawing near." Encouragement requires assembly. Similarly, Paul says that we are to be "teaching and admonishing one another in all wisdom, singing psalms and hymns and spiritual songs, with thankfulness in your hearts to God" (Col. 3:16). I have no way of teaching or admonishing someone if I am not with them, and vice versa! So attend church—Sundays especially, but other events throughout the week as you are able—so that you can give God the public worship that He deserves, and also so you can bless others and be blessed by others.

Submit

Membership requires that you take seriously the role that church leaders play. This is a humbling thing. To many, it's an *unattractive* thing. Why voluntarily put myself under the authority of other sinful, fallible humans? Well, because God tells us to: "Obey your leaders and submit to them, for they are keeping watch over your souls, as those who will have to give an account. Let them do this with joy and not with groaning, for that would be of no advantage to you" (Heb. 13:17). What the author of Hebrews is telling us here is that spiritual oversight is for our benefit. Your life will go better for you if you submit to the leadership of God-fearing, Bible-following men in the local church.

How can you show this submission? Pay attention to your pastor's messages. Take notes to help you follow along. If the elders offer instruction to you personally, consider it carefully and look to follow it. If they have called the congregation to meet both Sunday morning and Sunday evening, then go to both services! Speak well of your leaders to other people in the church. Find ways you can encourage them all in their labors. Don't cause problems in the church. Be an example to other people in how submission to authority can be a really good thing.

Pray

The church thrives on prayer. The New Testament saints "devoted themselves to … prayer" (Acts 2:42). Are you devoted to prayer? What about prayer for your church family? A faithful church member recognizes that an indispensable part of belonging to the church is interceding for the church. Here are some ways you can do that. Pray that the Lord would strengthen your pastor to preach God's Word accurately and clearly. Pray for the people who might be suffering. Pray that God would provide for the church, whatever her needs may be. Pray for the peace of the church (Ps. 122:6).

Give

One important way of showing your full commitment to the local church is by supporting it through financial contributions. In general, people's money will end up going towards the things they are passionate about. Christians should be passionate about the church, and church members indicate as much through intentional, regular giving to the local church. In the early church, the Lord's Day was a day where people would set aside some of their money to give to people in need or support pastors and missionaries. "Now concerning the collection for the saints: as I directed the churches of Galatia, so you also are to do. On the first day of every week, each of you is to put something aside and store it up, as he may prosper" (1 Cor. 16:1-2).

Paul's statement "as he may prosper" is critical. It means that there is not a set or predetermined number or percentage that we are to give to the church (see 2 Cor. 8:7). Rather, we are to give in proportion to how the Lord has blessed us. In terms of our financial situation, since the Lord has blessed us all in different ways, the *maximum* amount we can give will vary from believer to believer. In terms of our spiritual situation, since we have all equally received the lavish grace of Jesus Christ, there can be no *minimum* for us in our giving. The disposition of our heart should be, "I want to give everything I can to the God who gave everything to me!" As Paul writes, the gospel should motivate our giving: "For you know the grace of our Lord Jesus Christ, that though he was rich, yet for your sake he became poor, so that you by his poverty might become rich" (2 Cor. 8:9).

Serve

The ministry of the church is not allocated to just a select few, like the pastor, elders, or deacons, nor is it something that is allocated to one day of the week, but is constantly engaged. The church is not just an organization, but also an organism teeming with life. At least, it's meant to be! The whole congregation is called to the work of ministry, including you. To be a faithful member of the church, you should diligently seek areas that you can step up and offer a hand.

Sometimes people agonize over discovering their spiritual gift. The Bible does list some of them (look at 1 Corinthians 12, 14, and

Ephesians 4 for some examples). These lists are not meant to be exhaustive, so if none of them necessarily ring true for you, don't panic. Really, discovering and deploying your gifts in the church is as simple as a willingness to serve where there's a need. But what gifts we have, and how we should use them, can become such a contentious issue in church life that I think it's worth spending some more time on—so we will pick up the discussion in the next chapter.

MAIN POINT:

The Bible presents the local church as a discernible group of believers who must belong to one another through formal membership. Formal membership is not all we are after; we want faithful membership as well, which entails regular attendance, humble submission, earnest prayer, sacrificial stewardship, and loving service.

QUESTIONS FOR REFLECTION:

- Are you a member of a church? Why or why not?
- Do you regularly attend the activities of your church?
- What are some ways you could pray for your church?

7. A Healthy Body

We all know that keeping our bodies healthy is important. In fact, more than this, we all know *how* to keep our bodies healthy: diet, exercise, and sleep are vital components of keeping our systems working properly. So why do we still eat junk food, spend hours in front of the computer or TV, and get far too little sleep? Keeping our bodies healthy is hard work!

Keeping the church healthy takes work, too—and that work involves you! The Bible uses a multitude of metaphors to bring to life the purpose, mission, and nature of the church, the most frequent of which is that of the body (see Eph. 1:23; 3:6; 4:4; 5:23; Col 1:18; 3:15). In 1 Corinthians 12, Paul gives his most extended teaching on the subject of the body of Christ, and it's all about how to keep this spiritual body healthy! This is a chapter about how, as a member of the church, you are to live, serve, and fellowship within the church community to best edify it. If you have a Bible nearby, it wouldn't be a bad idea just to read through that chapter before continuing. It won't take long. If not, I've made sure to include all the key verses below. Consider with me three things we need to remember if we want to help the church body function healthily.

I MATTER

The first thing to remember is this: *you matter*. On Tuesdays we take my son to taekwondo, and immediately after that, we take my daughter to soccer. Two very different sports, run by entirely different organizations, and yet each program starts in almost an identical way: the coach will gather the kids around and get them to repeat some sort of mantra for the day, a variation usually of, "I am strong," "I am confident, "I am talented," or "I can do this." We've all seen that sort of thing morph into nauseating therapeutic nonsense, but, in the right dose, it's very healthy. Especially at a formative age, the only way kids can be a positive contributor to their team or to their sport is if they think they actually have something to contribute!

A Healthy Body

Paul is sort of gathering the church around him now and getting them to go over those basics, too. He does so by picturing individual body parts pouting that they are not as cool or as seemingly important as other body parts. "If the foot should say, 'Because I am not a hand, I do not belong to the body,' that would not make it any less a part of the body. And if the ear should say, 'Because I am not an eye, I do not belong to the body,' that would not make it any less a part of the body." (vv. 15-16). Have you ever felt that way in church? Have you ever thought, if only I could serve as frequently as she does, if only I could contribute more meaningfully to Bible studies like the other people, if only I could pray as meaningfully as he does…? We think to ourselves: if only we were more like those other people we see, we would be more helpful, more useful, more needed in the life of the church.

And Paul's response to that way of thinking is to say, "You matter! If you were just the same as everyone else, that'd be like the body only being an eye"—a weird and creepy image (see v. 17)! We think an eyeball is important, and it is. But if an eyeball is only an eyeball, well—*then it's only an eyeball*. Without a brain there's nothing to process the images it receives. Without feet there is nothing to get you to that thing you're looking at. Without a mouth there is no way to tell other people what you have seen. An eye as an eye is not much of anything. It's certainly not a body. "If all were a single member, where would the body be?" (v. 19). The diversity of body parts is not a flaw to the body as a whole, it's essential to it. What makes a body a body is the unity of the diversity.

The same is true in the church: what makes it the church is the part you play. Whether you feel like it or not, you are essential. *Feeling* like you have a part to play is not the deciding factor in whether or not you have a part to play. As a Christian, you are part of the body of Christ: "Now you are the body of Christ and individually members of it" (v. 27). And Paul wants you to function like it. And that starts by recognizing you have something to offer. It starts with you saying, "I matter." Be done with envy, jealousy, and self-pity. In gratitude, recognize that the same undeserved grace and the same incalculable power that has gifted the most "impressive" person in the church has gifted you. You matter.

THEY MATTER

The second key to a healthy functioning church is the inverse of the first point. For the church to function well, I need to know I matter and, secondly, that everyone else matters, too. Just as there is no place for jealousy in the church, there is no place for derision or disdain either. Verse 21: "The eye cannot say to the hand, 'I have no need of you,' nor again the head to the feet, 'I have no need of you.'"

In the classic *Star Trek* series, a running gag among viewers were the "red shirts," otherwise known as expendable crewmen. They were background characters on the *USS Enterprise* whom the screenwriters could easily sacrifice to a villain, adding a sense of heightened drama to the show while never threatening the main cast. Since they served no real purpose, they could be easily written off. There are no "expendable crewmen" in the church. Paul says that even the seemingly weaker parts of the body are "indispensable" (v. 22).

So, for the church to be healthy, we must avoid cliques. We avoid any behavior that makes others feel unwelcomed or unimportant. We should listen to, consider, and even celebrate the perspectives and positions of others on a whole host of matters. As a young person, you must make a point to get to know older saints and learn from their wisdom. Conversely, find younger people that you can mentor and encourage. The age segregation that many churches default to is not biblical or beneficial. The health of the body of Christ depends on us making room for everyone to use their gifts and make their contribution and fellowship with one another. Anything less leads to division—or amputation! The proper attitude instead is to have a concern and appreciation for everyone in the church, "that there may be no division in the body, but that the members may have the same care for one another" (v. 25).

I might not think about my pinky toe all that much—but when I stub it, it's *all* I can think about. When it's in pain, my whole body is in pain. Likewise, "If one member suffers, all suffer together; if one member is honored, all rejoice together" (v. 26). In other words, the attitude of a healthy church member is this: "We're all in this together!" No matter one's age, ethnicity, socio-economic background, or education, they matter in the church. You can show that by spending time and forging friendships with them all.

LOVES MATTERS MOST

Something interesting happens at the very end of 1 Corinthians 12. After Paul has gone into great detail describing how the church should live and serve together in order to promote the greatest spiritual health, he says "I will show you a still more excellent way" than this (v. 31). That excellent way is expounded for us in the next chapter: it's the way of love. Leon Morris writes, "There is something higher than the greatest of all these gifts, and this is within the reach of the humblest and the most ordinary believer"—it's faith working through love (Gal. 5:6).[7]

As it turns out, love is the most important component in a healthy church. "If I speak in the tongues of men and of angels, but have not love, I am a noisy gong or a clanging cymbal … I am nothing." (1 Cor. 13:1-2). Love makes it so that our service is rendered for the right reason: to the praise of God's glory and for the good of our neighbor. Without love, it is simply an exercise in pride. The greatest gift becomes a hurt, not a help, to the church when used in a loveless manner. Conversely, even a

---

7 Leon Morris, *1 Corinthians* (Grand Rapids, MI: Eerdmans, 1985), 176.

humble gift becomes a higher one when done in love. Without love, the body of Christ will come to nothing. In love, the church can face the greatest trials, experience the sweetest joys, and form the deepest bonds.

MAIN POINT:
The key to a healthy, functioning church body is to remember that God has brought the church together, and He doesn't make mistakes. Everyone in the church has a place to serve for the good of others.

QUESTIONS FOR REFLECTION:
- Have you ever been jealous of other people in the church? If so, why? What do you think Paul would say to you about that?
- What do you think are your gifts, or ways you could serve in the church?
- What are some gifts that might seem to be unimportant or non-essential, and how can you better appreciate their usefulness in the church?

8. An Unfinished Work

I have attempted in this little book to set forth the wonders of the local church: its privileged position, its thrilling mission, its glorious worship, and the benefits of submitting to its leadership and servings its members. The church is truly the greatest place on earth, and I believe that with all my heart. However, I am not so naïve as to suggest it is perfect—or even anywhere close to it. I want to address the church's imperfections because a primary reason people walk away from the church is because of its failures and flaws. They are turned off by rank hypocrisy. They are deeply wounded by sin in the church and can't bear the thought of ever going back. What can we do to process that hurt, and still appreciate the church for what it is?

DO A REALITY CHECK

First, it's important to know that the Bible never presents a gilded picture of the church on earth. It never suggests that our experience in the people of God is going to be only sunshine and daisies. Actually, when you read the Bible, it is brutally honest about the failures and hardships of God's people. Sometimes it's embarrassing to read the sinful and stubborn things they do—and then shameful when we think of how we often do the same things! Think about the seven churches that Jesus addresses in the opening of Revelation. Of the seven, *only two* are not rebuked for wayward doctrine or practice (way to go Smyrna and Philadelphia!). The church is a flawed place, but the Bible never suggested otherwise. In fact, if it were not so, we would hardly have a New Testament, since many epistles are written to sort out issues in congregations.

The Bible also warns of the presence of enemies inside the church. Paul warns the Ephesians that "fierce wolves will come in among you, not sparing the flock" (Acts 20:29; see also Matt 7:15). If you have experienced mistreatment or misdirection from a leader in the church, I am terribly sorry. The fact that some intentionally use their positions of influence to do harm is one of the greatest evils of all. But the Jesus who warned of false pastors also said He would give true pastors as a gift to His church (Eph. 4:11). Don't give up on the church because of past hurt from the church. As bizarre as it sounds, the church is the only place that can heal you from past hurt. Remember, it has the means of grace. It has the means by which God will comfort your heart with the blessings that are found in Jesus Christ.

So, part of the solution here is simply to recognize that the church is going to be a messy place. Go in with your eyes wide open, but your heart open, too. Don't expect more out of the church than she can offer, but what she can offer receive in faith and love.

THANK GOD FOR HOSPITALS

Viewed in a different light, the foibles of the imperfect church should be one of the greatest inducements to join it. Where else would sinners like you and me be welcomed but in a place that is filled with other sinners? For the church to be perfect, God would have to permit in only the righteous—which would be to effectively bar the doors permanently! The mess of sin in the church is a sign that it's a place for sinners.

Imagine a friend of yours suffers a tremendous head wound while the two of you are playing basketball. They are bleeding really badly, so you say you will take them to the emergency room. What would you say if they replied, "No, I don't want to go to the emergency room. There's too much blood there, and there's a lot of noise from people moaning and crying." You would rightly respond, "Exactly! That's why you need to go there! That's where bleeding, crying people go!" You would be even more exasperated if they countered, "No, really. I think the better thing would be to go get some ice cream." Ice cream might be enjoyable, but it will not help the serious injury that needs to be addressed.

Sadly, this is the kind of logic people use for staying away from church. They don't want to go because of the presence of sin, all the while forgetting the presence of sin in their own hearts is precisely why they need to go! Instead, what do people do with their sin? They try to numb themselves to its effects through entertainment, or distract themselves through work—sort of like getting ice cream when you need to be at the hospital. Others punish themselves by wallowing in guilt or shame—all the while the key to peace and joy is found in the church, freely offered to all who will come.

The church is not for perfect people. It's for people who know they're not perfect. Or we could say it's the perfect place for imperfect people! Rather than demean the church because it makes mistakes or causes hurt, we should rejoice that the Lord has provided a society for people who make mistakes and cause hurt—a place for us! And it's not just a safe place for self-professed sinners; it's a transformative place. It's where we can come to receive the Lord's forgiveness and to be changed.

THINK ABOUT JESUS

It is not without deep significance that the person who was hurt the most by the church never gave up on her. It was the people of God, not the world, that crucified Jesus. If anyone should have a reason to walk out on the church and never come back it would be Christ. And yet there is nothing Jesus loves more in all the world, second only to the Father and the Holy Spirit, than His church. It's a breathtaking thought about the mercy, love, and faithfulness of the Lord.

CHURCH

If you have been burned by the church in the past and are tempted to leave (or you have left and are not inclined to come back), I would encourage you to think about Jesus. The Bible tells us Jesus is an example to us for how we should live the Christian life. He is certainly more than that, but He is not less. Though not initially written regarding difficulties within the church, this word from Hebrews is fitting advice: "Consider him who endured from sinners such hostility against himself, so that you may not grow weary or fainthearted" (Heb. 12:3).

The argument here is from the greater to the lesser. If Jesus could endure the cross, surely we can endure the sufferings that will come our way! In other words, look at the faithfulness of Christ to shore up your own fidelity. Find the strength you need to endure the offense and heartache that might come in church life by considering how Jesus responded in a far worse situation. That's what Paul tells the Colossian congregation: "Put on then, as God's chosen ones, holy and beloved, compassionate hearts, kindness, humility, meekness, and patience, bearing with one another and, if one has a complaint against another, forgiving each other; as the Lord has forgiven you, so you also must forgive" (Col. 3:12-13).

KEEP YOUR HOPE IN HEAVEN

While the presence of sin among God's people is discouraging, it's also a helpful corrective for us. It is a persistent reminder that the church here on earth has not reached the goal and cannot be our hope in this life. There is more to the story yet to be written. The flaws of the church remind us that there is something much better promised to us very soon, and to look for it in the right place: "But our citizenship is in heaven, and from it we await a Savior, the Lord Jesus Christ, who will transform our lowly body to be like his glorious body, by the power that enables him even to subject all things to himself" (Phil. 3:20-21). So the church, like everything else on earth, is imperfect. But unlike anything else on earth, one day it won't be.

The majority of the time I lived in Philadelphia, the famous Independence Hall was undergoing renovations and there was scaffolding obscuring the front of it. Although this was a disappointing eyesore in the heart of the historic district, we all knew the scaffolding would one day be taken down and the building would be even more beautiful for it. That's kind of like the church right now. There is sin and suffering that mars the full beauty of the church, but God even uses this to produce in us our future glory (Rom. 8:18). Therefore, we have every reason to press on in worship, fellowship, and ministry, and to do so with hopeful confidence that no amount of sin or setback can defeat God's people. John writes, "Beloved, we are God's children now, and what we will be has not yet appeared; but we know that when he appears we shall be like him, because we shall see him as he is. And everyone who thus hopes in him purifies himself as he is pure" (1 John 3:2-3; see also Rev. 19).

Since that is where the church will be one day, the church is where you need to be *right now*. It is to His people and His people only that God has promised glorification. So, we bear and forbear with the failures and weaknesses of the church. We humbly acknowledge that sometimes we cause them, even! But we don't give up on the church. We don't blame the church for sin. We rejoice that the church is a place for sinners, and the place where sinners will one day become sinless saints:

"he who began a good work in you will bring it to completion at the day of Jesus Christ" (Phil. 1:6). The words of John Newton in regard to personal sanctification are apt for describing the church as well: "I am not what I ought to be, I am not what I want to be, I am not what I hope to be in another world; but still I am not what I once used to be, and by the grace of God I am what I am." The church isn't perfect but, by the grace of God, it's still the perfect place for you.

MAIN POINT:
The church is a flawed place, but that's actually one of its greatest features. It's a place where all sinners are welcome to receive forgiveness in Christ and the promise of future glorification.

QUESTIONS FOR REFLECTION:
- Have you ever been hurt by someone in the church? If so, how did you respond? How should you respond?
- What does it mean that the person who was hurt the most by the church never gave up on her?
- What might you say to someone who dismisses the church out of hand because they think it's filled with hypocrites?

Appendix A: Next Steps

What do we do now? Once you get a grasp on the basics of the church, a few next steps are essential:
- Go to church! You might already be doing that—great. If not, start this Sunday.
- If you are not already, become a member of a local church. Submit to the authority and leadership of elders who will get to know you and care for your soul. Ask them what steps are needed to make this happen.
- Ask the Lord to help you see how you can serve in your local church.
- Continue to search the Scripture for what it says about belonging to the body of Christ, and apply that to your life.
- Pray for the peace and prosperity of the church, wherever she gathers.

Appendix B: Other Books on this Topic

Dustin Benge, *The Loveliest Place: The Beauty and Glory of the Church* (Wheaton: Crossway, 2022)

Jonathan Landry Cruse, *Church Membership* (Blessings of the Faith; Phillipsburg: P&R, 2024)

Mark Dever, *What is a Healthy Church?* (Second Edition; Wheaton: Crossway, 2024)

> I would also commend the rest of the 9Marks *Building Healthy Churches* series for a number of great, short, accessible books about the local church.

Mark G. Johnston, *The Church: Glorious Body, Radiant Bride* (Edinburgh: Banner of Truth, 2018)

CHURCH

Jeremy Linneman, *Why Do We Feel Lonely at Church?* (Wheaton: Crossway, 2023)

Harrison Perkins, *A Student's Guide to Living Out Reformed Theology* (Track; Fearn: Christian Focus, 2024)

Philip Graham Ryken, *City on a Hill* (Chicago: Moody, 2003)

Stephen Smallman, *What Is a Reformed Church?* (Phillipsburg: P&R, 2012)

*Also available from
Christian Focus Publications
and Reformed Youth Ministries ...*

TRACK CULTURE

SHARON JAMES

SERIES EDITED BY
JOHN PERRITT

A STUDENT'S GUIDE TO WORLDVIEW

978-1-5271-0843-1

Track: Culture

A Student's Guide to Worldview

Sharon James

Is there a view that's true?

We all view the world through a certain lens. Depending on our upbringing, geography, experiences, and a whole host of other influences, we will see life a certain way.

We all care about truth, justice, love, good and evil. Our understanding of these values is shaped by what we hear and are taught. Yet, unbeknownst to many in society, the fruit that culture claims, is rooted in Christianity.

By walking through historical overviews and sharing real-life stories, Sharon James teaches readers how to read culture through the lens of scripture. This introduction will equip the next generation with the wisdom needed to think through some of the most divisive cultural issues of our day.

978-1-5271-1177-6

Track: Christian Life

A Student's Guide to Grief

Paul Tautges

The reality of death means that we all encounter grief at some point in our lives. But what does the Bible say about how we handle the aftermath of separation? Paul Tautges compassionately addresses the struggles we face when dealing with loss, all the while pointing to the hope and comfort that can be found in Christ.

Biblical Comfort: Explore the timeless wisdom of scripture and find solace in knowing the God who grieves. Track: Grief gently guides you through biblical passages that provide strength, reassurance, and the promise of God's eternal love during times of sorrow.

Practical Tools: Track: Grief equips you with practical tools to navigate the grieving process with grace. Engage with the thought-provoking questions in each chapter, and prayer through what you read, and learn to rely on God, even when navigating the challenging terrain of grief.

HARRISON PERKINS

SERIES EDITED BY JOHN PERRITT

TRACK: DOCTRINE

A STUDENT'S GUIDE TO LIVING OUT REFORMED THEOLOGY

978-1-5271-1147-9

Track: Doctrine

A Student's Guide to Living Out Reformed Theology

Harrison Perkins

Huh? What exactly do you mean by that…

Harrison Perkins, a senior research fellow for the Craig Centre for the Study of the Westminster Standards, introduces us to some of the main themes of Reformed theology in this addition to the Track series.

Starting with its principal foundations – the grace and love of God – Harrison goes on to tackle some of the trickier aspects of Reformed theology, such as predestination. With a clear and comprehendible explanation, he demonstrates how these doctrines apply to the life of the believer.

Get the whole set of *Track* books:

Doctrine:
A Student's Guide to...
- *Apologetics*
- *Living Out Reformed Theology*
- *Justification*
- *Sanctification*
- *Glorification*
- *Missions*
- *Scripture*
- *Church*

Culture:
A Student's Guide to...
- *The Power of Story*
- *Navigating Culture*
- *Worldview*
- *Technology*
- *Social Media*
- *Gaming*
- *Politics*

Visit christianfocus.com

Christian Life:
A Student's Guide to...
- *Reading and Applying the Bible*
- *Grief*
- *Body Image*
- *Purity in a Porn-Satured Culture*
- *Depression*
- *Anxiety*
- *Dating, Marriage, and Sex*
- *Womanhood*
- *Rest*

Reformed Youth Ministries (RYM) exists to serve the Church in reaching and equipping youth for Christ. Over the last five decades RYM has grown from a single summer conference into three areas of ministry:

- **Conferences:** RYM hosts multiple summer conferences for local church groups in a variety of locations across the United States.
- **Training:** Youth Leader Training (YLT) is for anyone serving with youth in the local church. RYM also offers a Church Internship Program in partnering local churches, youth leader coaching and youth ministry consulting services.
- **Resources:** RYM offers a growing array of resources for leaders, parents, and students.

RYM is a 501(c)(3) non-profit organization. To learn more or to partner with RYM in reaching and equipping the next generation for Christ please visit rym.org.

Christian Focus Publications

Our mission statement
Staying Faithful

In dependence upon God we seek to impact the world through literature faithful to His infallible Word, the Bible. Our aim is to ensure that the Lord Jesus Christ is presented as the only hope to obtain forgiveness of sin, live a useful life and look forward to heaven with Him.

Our Books are published in four imprints:

CHRISTIAN FOCUS

Popular works including biographies, commentaries, basic doctrine and Christian living.

MENTOR

Books written at a level suitable for Bible College and seminary students, pastors, and other serious readers. The imprint includes commentaries, doctrinal studies, examination of current issues and church history.

CHRISTIAN HERITAGE

Books representing some of the best material from the rich heritage of the church.

CF4KIDS

Children's books for quality Bible teaching and for all age groups: Sunday school curriculum, puzzle and activity books; personal and family devotional titles, biographies and inspirational stories – because you are never too young to know Jesus!

Christian Focus Publications Ltd,
Geanies House, Fearn, Ross-shire,
IV20 1TW, Scotland, United Kingdom.
www.christianfocus.com